GW00367205

Theory of Music Workbook

for Trinity Guildhall written examinations

Grade 2

by Naomi Yandell

Published by:
Trinity College London
89 Albert Embankment
London SE1 7TP UK

T +44 (0)20 7820 6100
F +44 (0)20 7820 6161
E music@trinityguildhall.co.uk
www.trinityguildhall.co.uk

Designer and editor: Natasha Witts
Music processed by New Notations London
Printed in England by Halstan & Co. Ltd, Amersham, Bucks

Grade 2 Theory of Music Syllabus from 2007

Section 1	General multiple choice – 10 questions	(10 marks)
Section 2	Writing scales, arpeggios, broken chords	(20 marks)
Section 3	Correcting mistakes	(10 marks)
Section 4	Sequence	(10 marks)
Section 5	Transposition	(15 marks)
Section 6	Writing a tune to a given rhythm	(15 marks)
Section 7	Analysis – 10 questions	(20 marks)

Questions and tasks may cover all matters specified in Grade 1 and also the following:

Rhythm

1. Note values of dotted crotchets, single quavers and semiquavers (beamed in 4s only) using English terms (with an option to use American terms, e.g. minim or half note)
2. Rest values of dotted crotchets, single quavers using English terms (with an option to use American terms, e.g. minim or half note rest)
3. Time signatures of $\frac{3}{8}$, $\frac{2}{2}$ or $\mathsf{C}\!\!\!|$, and $\frac{3}{2}$
4. Grouping note and rest values above within $\frac{3}{8}$, $\frac{2}{2}$ (split or cut common time) or $\frac{3}{2}$ (excluding semiquavers except where grouped in 4s)
5. Tied notes
6. Concept of slow and fast beats being possible in different time signatures (e.g. $\frac{3}{8}$ can be slow and $\frac{2}{2}$ can be fast) as shown by tempo indications and metronome markings
7. Syncopation [♪♩♪ and/or ♩♩♩ patterns only]

Pitch

1. Naming and using notes in treble or bass clefs (to two leger lines above or below the stave)
2. Related keys, major/minor and vice versa
3. A, D and E minor keys, their natural (Aeolian mode) and harmonic minor scales, key signatures, one-octave arpeggios and tonic triads
4. First inversions of major and minor tonic triads of keys covered so far (and an understanding of the terms root position and first inversion)
5. Identifying the key of a piece in A, D or E minor
6. Concept of numbers 1-8 being used to name degrees of the minor scale
7. 1st degree of the minor scale being known as the tonic
8. Degrees of the minor scale can be at different registers
9. Minor tonic triad labelled:
   – as a chord symbol above the music (e.g. Am in the key of A minor)
   – as a Roman numeral below the music (e.g. i in the key of A minor)
10. Intervals (unison, major/minor 2nd, major/minor 3rd, perfect 4ths, 5ths and octaves above any tonic for the grade)
11. Circle of 5ths relating to the keys above
12. Broken chords
13. Sequences
14. Ranges of soprano, alto, tenor and bass voices
15. Transposing a tune up or down an octave within a clef (treble or bass)

Musical words and symbols

Dynamic and articulation marks
Decrescendo, phrase marks, *tenuto* (and signs and abbreviations for these where appropriate)

Tempo, expression marks and other words and signs
Adagio, *allegretto*, *cantabile*, *espressivo*, first and second time bars, *grazioso*, metronome marks, *molto*, octave signs, pause mark, *vivace* (and signs and abbreviations for these where appropriate)

Introduction

Using this workbook

The writing in the boxes [   ] tells you:

- About the music that you sing, or play on your instrument

- What you need to know to pass your Trinity Guildhall Grade 2 Theory of Music examination. Topics from the previous grade should also be known

Doing the tasks

- Use a pencil with a sharp point and a fairly soft lead so that you can easily rub out what you have written if you need to

- Be careful to be accurate with musical notes and signs – this will make a difference to your marks because the examiner must be able to read what you have written

- Read through the boxes to make sure you understand how to do the tasks and ask for help if you need it

- The first task in each section has usually been done for you in green to show you what to do

- Use the picture of the piano keyboard on page 59. It is there to help you, even if you do not play a keyboard instrument

- **Always try to play, sing or tap the music you write.** This is a very important part of learning, and will help you 'hear' what you write in your head. It will help you in the examination when you have to work in silence

What comes next?

When you have finished this book try some sample papers. You can download them from www.trinityguildhall.co.uk (follow the links to Theory from the Music page). You will then be ready to ask your teacher to enter you for the Grade 2 Theory of Music examination.

Acknowledgements

Trinity Guildhall would like to acknowledge the invaluable contribution to the development of this music theory programme by music teachers, professors, examiners, language specialists and students from around the world. Their comments have usefully informed the final shape of the workbooks and examination papers, and are much appreciated.

New notes for Grade 2

Here, in green are the new treble clef note names you need to know for Grade 2. You know the others from Grade 1.

G A B Middle C D E F G A B C D E F G A B C D

1 Name these notes:

G ___ ___ ___ ___ ___ ___ ___

Handy tip!

Leger lines are written the same distance away from the stave as the stave lines.

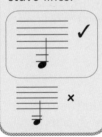

2 Write three different **D naturals**.

3 Write three different **C sharps**.

Handy tip!

Place leger-line accidentals carefully so that they belong to the correct notes.

4 Write three different **A flats**.

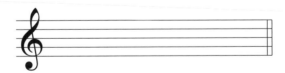

5 Write three different **G naturals**.

6 Write three different **B flats**.

7 Write three different **G sharps**.

New notes for Grade 2 𝄢

Here, in green are the new bass clef note names you need to know for Grade 2. You know the others from Grade 1.

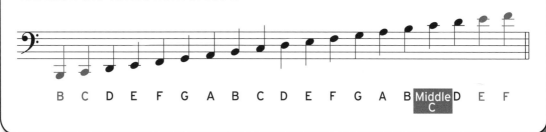

B C D E F G A B C D E F G A B Middle C D E F

1 Name these notes:

B _ _ _ _ _ _

2 Write three different **B naturals**.

3 Write three different **C sharps**.

Handy tip!

Test yourself by writing out every Grade 2 note on a separate sheet of paper and timing how quickly you can name each one.

All notes can be checked using the **G** in the G clef (𝄞), the **F** in the F clef (𝄢) or **Middle C.**

4 Write three different **E flats**.

5 Write three different **F naturals**.

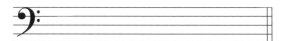

6 Write three different **F sharps**.

7 Write three different **D naturals**.

Note values

Here are the new note values for Grade 2:

1. The **single quaver**: ♪

Quavers (whether single or beamed together) last for half a crotchet beat each.

2. The **dotted crotchet**: ♩.

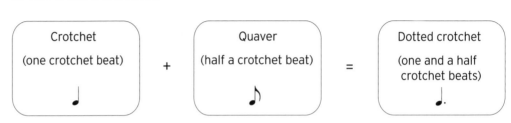

Crotchet		Quaver		Dotted crotchet
(one crotchet beat)	+	(half a crotchet beat)	=	(one and a half crotchet beats)
♩		♪		♩.

The dotted crotchet is often followed by a single quaver because together they make up two crotchet beats:

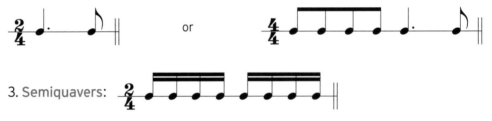

3. Semiquavers:

A semiquaver lasts for a quarter of a crotchet beat. For Grade 2 semiquavers are always beamed together in groups of four where the beat is a crotchet.

1 Add the total number of crotchet beats in these note values.

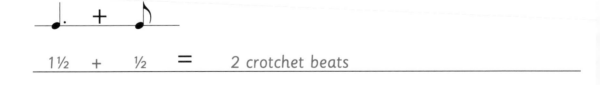

1½ + ½ = 2 crotchet beats

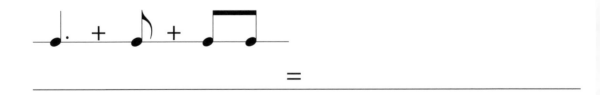

=

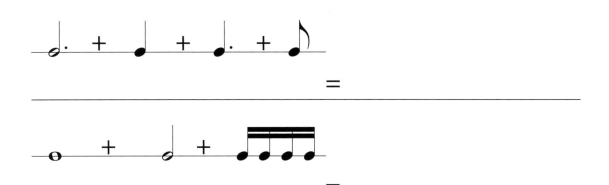

= _____

= _____

2 Fill the coloured boxes with correctly grouped quavers to complete the bars.

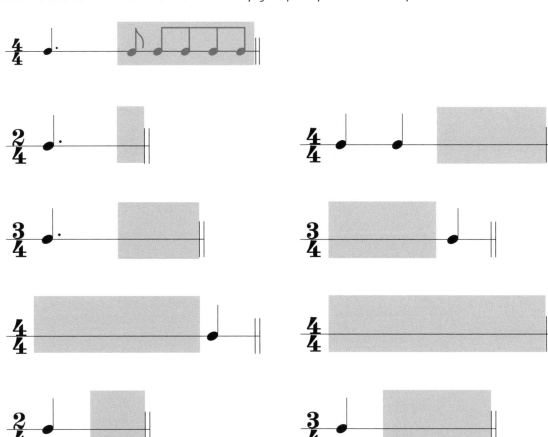

3 Write a dotted crotchet at the beginning of each bar and complete it with single quavers and/or crotchets.

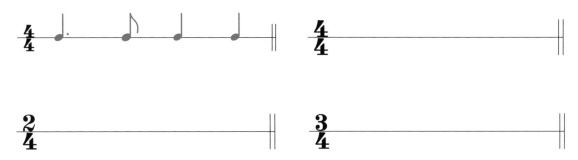

4 Write 4-bar rhythms using the note values you know.

Ties

Sometimes composers want musicians to play notes that are not of a standard length. To do this they 'tie' same-pitch notes together to make longer notes.

Here is an **F** that lasts for eight crotchet beats. Notice that the note is tied across the bar line:

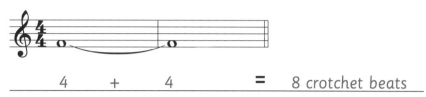

4 + 4 = 8 crotchet beats

Ties are usually used only where it is not possible to use a standard note:

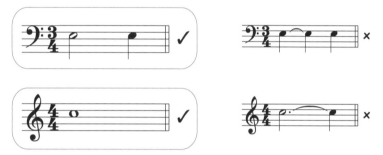

If a tied note has an accidental before it, that accidental applies to all the notes that are tied together, even if they are tied across a bar line. For example, this tied **F sharp** lasts for four crotchet beats:

Handy tip!

Put ties close to the note-heads and away from the stems. They should not quite touch the note-heads that they are tying together. If you are tying a dotted note to another note, begin the tie just after the dot.

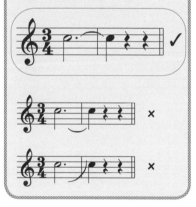

1 Add the total number of crotchet beats in these tied notes.

2 + 2 + 2 + 1 = 7 crotchet beats

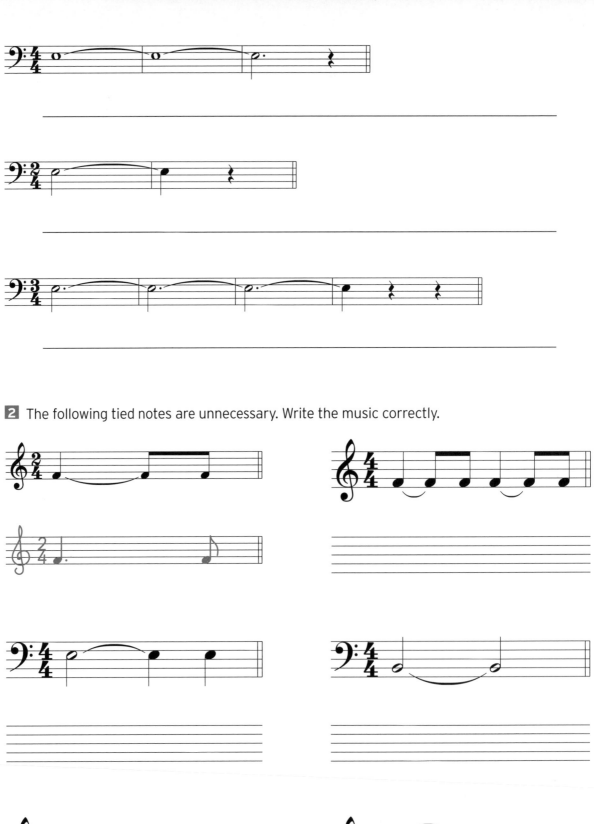

2 The following tied notes are unnecessary. Write the music correctly.

Handy tip!

Sometimes tied notes are carried over to the next line of music:

3 Look at the following music and add ties where possible.

There is no need to tie rests together. The silence just continues:

4 + 2 = silence lasting for 6 crotchet beats

4 Add the total number of crotchet beats of silence in these rests.

_____

_____

Remember

A semibreve rest is used to show a whole bar of silence in any time signature.

_____

_____

9

The quaver rest

The only new rest for Grade 2 is the **quaver rest**: ✲

Where the beat in a bar is a crotchet, this rest is only written if there is no other quaver rest within the same crotchet beat.

If a dotted crotchet's worth of silence is needed, always complete one crotchet beat with a rest before beginning the next:

This applies to all time signatures with a crotchet beat.

1 Fill in the coloured boxes with correctly grouped rests to complete the bars.

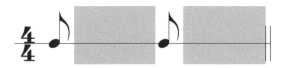

2 Write 4-bar rhythms using the note and rest values you know.
Include at least three rests in every rhythm.

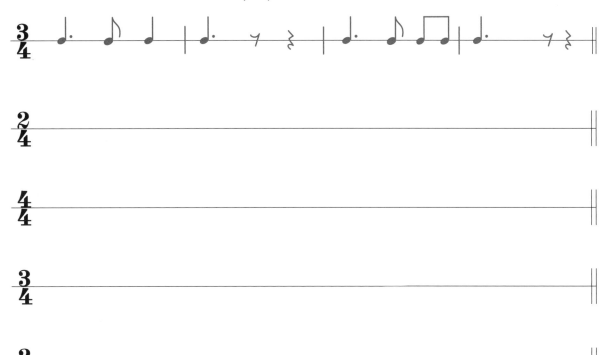

3 The following music contains mistakes in the grouping of notes and rests.
Write it out correctly.

New time signatures

Every time signature that you have learned so far has a **4** at the bottom, showing that you should count in crotchet beats.

This is not always the case. Look at this:

$\frac{3}{8}$

The top number of a time signature shows the number of beats in a bar

The bottom number shows the type of beat in a bar
(8 means quaver)

In $\frac{3}{8}$ there are three quaver beats in the bar. Here notes and rests are usually grouped in quaver beats except where three quaver notes appear in a bar – then they are beamed together to make the music easy to read.

Use two quaver rests where there are two quaver beats of silence in $\frac{3}{8}$.

Remember

In all time signatures, you should use ties only where it is not possible to use a standard note.

or C

In or **C** there are two minim beats in the bar. Here notes and rests are usually grouped in minim beats.

Number of beats in a bar

Type of beat in a bar (2 means minim)

Did you know?

Composers tend to use $\frac{4}{4}$ or **C** where they want a feeling of four in a bar and $\frac{2}{2}$ or **C** when they want a feeling of two in a bar. Grouping notes and rests in $\frac{4}{4}$ is very similar to $\frac{2}{2}$.

 ✓

✗

 ✓

✗

✗

$\frac{3}{2}$

Like $\frac{2}{2}$, $\frac{3}{2}$ is counted in minim beats. Notes and rests are usually grouped in minim beats.

A full bar's note in $\frac{3}{2}$ is 𝅝·

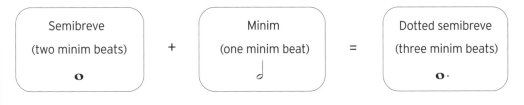

Semibreve (two minim beats)		Minim (one minim beat)		Dotted semibreve (three minim beats)
𝅝	+	𝅗𝅥	=	𝅝·

1 Write the correct number of beats (quavers, crotchets or minims) in each of the following bars.

2 Fill the coloured boxes with correctly grouped notes to complete the bars.

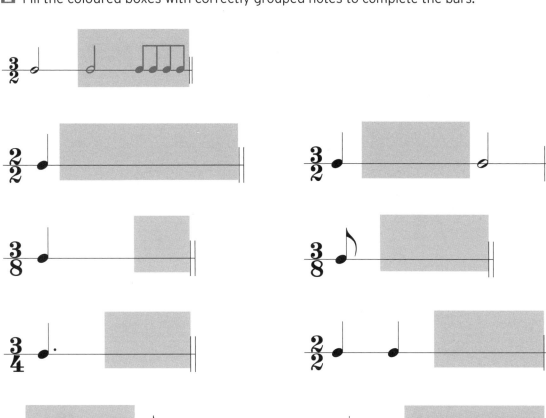

Remember

Always complete one beat with a note or rest before you go onto the next, working from the beginning of the bar. Think in the main beat of the bar (quaver, crotchet or minim).

3 Fill the coloured boxes with correctly grouped rests to complete the bars.

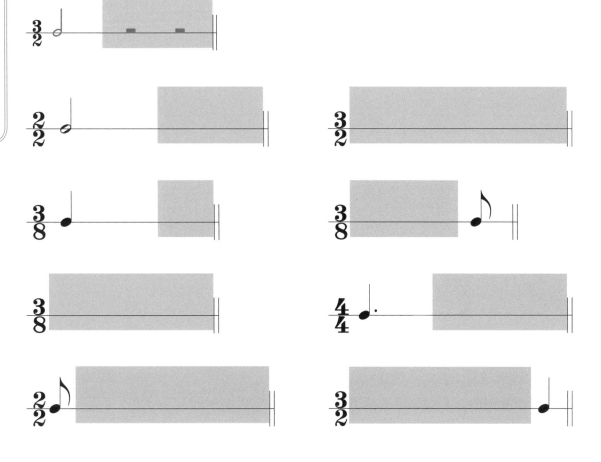

4 Look at the following music. Add bar lines to agree with the time signatures.

5 Write 4-bar rhythms using the note and rest values you know. Include at least three rests in every rhythm.

6 The following music contains mistakes in the grouping of notes and rests.
Write it out correctly.

Sousa

Rachmaninov

© Copyright 1908, 1921 Hawkes & Son (London) Ltd. Reproduced by permission of Boosey and Hawkes Music Publishers Ltd.

Cabezón

Schubert

Tartini

Slow and fast beats

Handy tip!

Look at page 48 for the new musical words and symbols for Grade 2.

The tempo marking at the beginning of a piece usually tells the player whether the speed of the beat (quaver, crotchet or minim) is slow or fast. A piece in $\frac{3}{8}$ can be very slow if marked **Adagio**, while a piece in $\frac{2}{2}$ can be very fast indeed if marked **Allegro molto**.

Some composers use metronome markings to give the exact speed of the beat (quaver, crotchet or minim). These markings tell the player how many quaver, crotchet or minim beats there are per minute.

M.M. ♩ = 100 – means 100 minim beats per minute

M.M. ♩ = 100 – means 100 crotchet beats per minute

1 Arrange the metronome markings in order of the speed of the beat.

Did you know?

M.M. is short for Maelzel's Metronome. M.M. is usually left out so that the marking is written like this: ♩ = 60. Players bear these markings in mind but often don't play at the exact speed indicated.

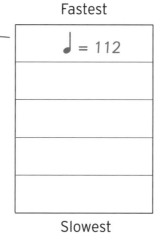

M.M. ♩ = 60

M.M. ♩ = 100

M.M. ♩ = 48

M.M. ♩ = 72

M.M. ♩ = 112

Fastest

♩ = 112

Slowest

2 Arrange the metronome markings in order of the speed of the beat.

M.M. ♩ = 132

M.M. ♩ = 120

M.M. ♩ = 60

M.M. ♩ = 148

M.M. ♩ = 48

Fastest

Slowest

3 Arrange the metronome markings in order of the speed of the beat (quaver, crotchet or minim).

Fastest

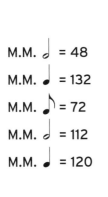

M.M. ♪ = 60

M.M. 𝅗𝅥 = 72

M.M. ♩ = 84

M.M. ♪ = 48

M.M. 𝅗𝅥 = 112

Slowest

4 Arrange the metronome markings in order of the speed of the beat (quaver, crotchet or minim).

Fastest

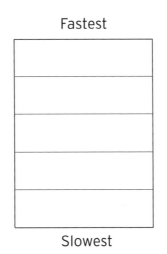

M.M. 𝅗𝅥 = 48

M.M. ♩ = 132

M.M. ♪ = 72

M.M. 𝅗𝅥 = 112

M.M. ♩ = 120

Slowest

5 Tick the line of music with the fastest beat per minute (quaver, crotchet or minim).

Adagio ♪ = 66

Allegro 𝅗𝅥 = 120

Andante ♩ = 76

19

Syncopation

Instead of writing music on the usual beats of the bar, sometimes composers 'throw' notes offbeat (before or after the beat). This is called **syncopation** and has been popular with composers writing in many different styles.

These are the two syncopated patterns that you need to recognise for Grade 2:

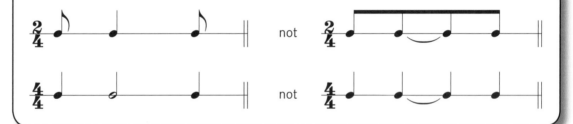

Look at the way they are written; they break the normal rules for grouping notes.

 1 Write two more repeats of these syncopated ostinati.

2 Write 4-bar rhythms using the note and rest values you know.
Include at least one syncopated pattern.

Relative minors and majors

Just as you have close relatives in your family, so major keys have keys that are closely related. The closest minor key to each major key is its **relative minor**. They share a key signature – just as people share characteristics with their families.

As you know from Grade 1, the key of C major has no sharps or flats in its key signature.

Likewise the relative minor key of C major has no sharps or flats in its key signature.

1 Using your knowledge of the major keys from Grade 1, write out the key signatures for their relative minor keys:

Key signature of G major:

Key signature of G major's relative minor key:

Key signature of C major:

Key signature of C major's relative minor key:

Key signature of F major:

Key signature of F major's relative minor key:

Finding the tonic of a relative minor key

Remember

A semitone means 'half a tone'. There is a distance of a semitone between every next-door note on the keyboard — black or white.

Count **down** three semitones from the tonic of a major key to find the tonic of its relative minor key, for example:

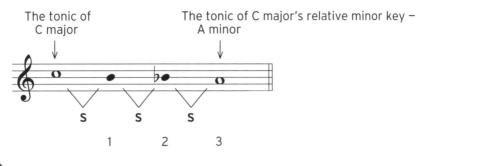

1 Count **down** three semitones to find the tonic of each relative minor.

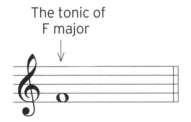
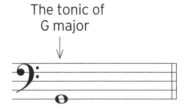
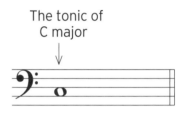

Finding the tonic of a relative major key

Count **up** three semitones from the tonic of a minor key to find the tonic of the relative major key, for example:

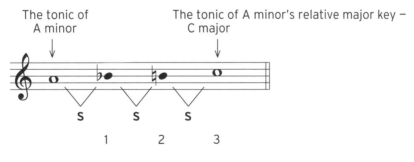

1 Count **up** three semitones to find the tonic of each relative major.

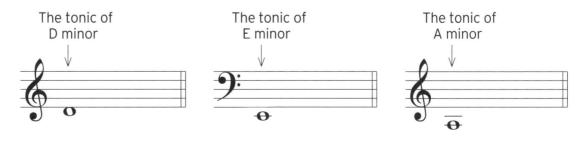

Minor keys

Did you know?

People often say that music in a major key feels happy and that music in a minor key feels sad. See what you think by playing two pieces, one in a major key and one in a minor key.

Why minor keys sound different from major keys

If someone tells you that a piece of music is **in the key of A minor**, it means that the music you hear will mostly use the notes from the scale of A minor.

Within any key, the 1st degree of the scale (whatever the register) is the **tonic**. Tunes often begin and end on it with the result that the tonic sounds special.

In Grade 1 you learned that in any major scale semitones appear only between the 3rd & 4th and 7th & 8th degrees of the scale.

Minor keys sound different from major keys mainly because the tone-semitone pattern is different.

There are several versions of the minor scale tone-semitone pattern. For Grade 2 you need to know about **natural** *and* **harmonic** minor scales.

The natural minor scale

The **natural minor scale** is the simplest kind of minor scale and is used a lot in folk and jazz. If you play all the white notes on a keyboard – not from **C** to **C** as for the scale of C major, but from its relative minor tonic **A** to **A** – you will be playing A natural minor scale.

Here it is going up:

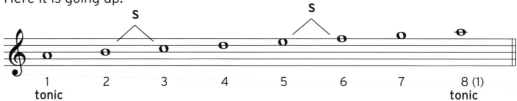

And going down:

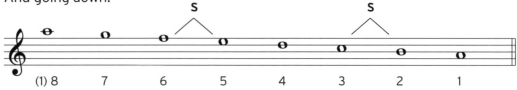

Remember

The 1st degree of the scale (major or minor) is called the **tonic**.

The notes are exactly the same as for the C major scale. However, the tonic note is **A** not **C**, which gives a different focus to the music.

In every natural minor scale this tone-semitone pattern is the same.

24

1 Give a name for the 1st degree in any key (major or minor).

Tonic

2 Which note is the tonic in the key of A minor?

3 If you write a piece in the key of A minor, from which scale will you take most of the notes?

4 If you listen to a piece in the key of A minor, on which note will the music often begin and end?

5 Write the tonic in two different registers in the key of A minor.

6 Write the tonic in three different registers in the key of C major.

> **Handy tip!**
> Write in the degrees of the scale if you find it useful so that you can check that there is a distance of a semitone between the 2nd & 3rd and the 5th & 6th degrees.

7 Write a one-octave A natural minor scale in semibreves going up.

8 Write a one-octave A natural minor scale in minims going down.

9 Write a one-octave A natural minor scale in semibreves going up.

10 Write a one-octave A natural minor scale in minims going down.

The harmonic minor scale

The **harmonic minor scale** is the same as the natural minor scale except that the pitch of the 7th degree is raised by a semitone (going up and going down). This means that there is a wide interval of a tone plus a semitone between the 6th & 7th degrees of the harmonic minor scale and semitones between the 2nd & 3rd, 5th & 6th and 7th & 8th degrees.

Here is A harmonic minor scale going up:

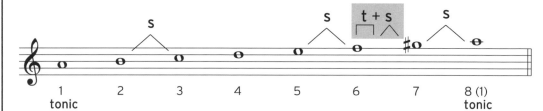

And going down:

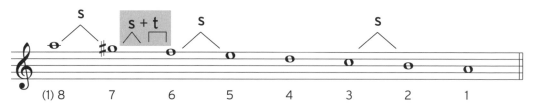

In every harmonic minor scale this tone-semitone pattern is the same.

1 Raise the 7th degree by a semitone each time to change these scales from A natural minor scale to A harmonic minor scale.

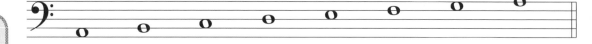

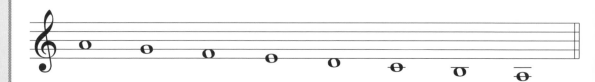

2 Write a one-octave A harmonic minor scale in minims going down.

Intervals – major and minor 3rds

In Grade 1 you learned that an interval means the distance between two notes.

Just to remind you, here are two intervals of a 3rd:

Interval: <u>3rd</u>

Interval: <u>3rd</u>

Although they are both 3rds, there is a small (but important) difference. (It's a little like tea and coffee – they are both drinks, but different kinds.)

For Grade 2 you need to know the difference between a **major 3rd** and a **minor 3rd** and label them like this:

Interval: <u>Major 3rd</u>

Interval: <u>Minor 3rd</u>

In major keys there is always an interval of a major 3rd between the 1st and 3rd degrees of the scale:

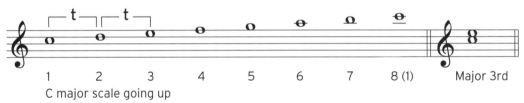

| 1 | 2 | 3 | 4 | 5 | 6 | 7 | 8 (1) | Major 3rd |

C major scale going up

In minor keys there is always an interval of a minor 3rd between the 1st and 3rd degrees of the scale:

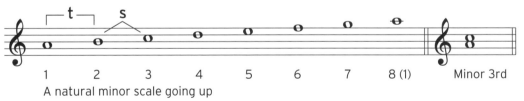

| 1 | 2 | 3 | 4 | 5 | 6 | 7 | 8 (1) | Minor 3rd |

A natural minor scale going up

The different interval between the 1st and 3rd degrees of major and minor scales is part of the reason that they have a different character.

1 Label the following scales. Then write the 1st and 3rd degrees of each scale as an interval and name it.

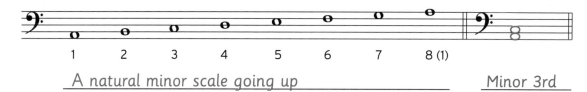

1   2   3   4   5   6   7   8 (1)

A natural minor scale going up   Minor 3rd

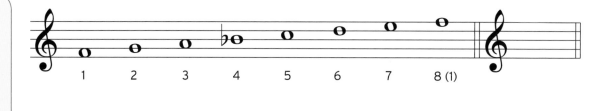

1   2   3   4   5   6   7   8 (1)

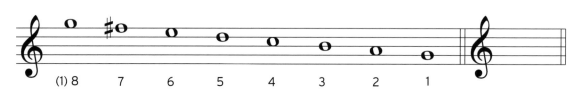

(1) 8   7   6   5   4   3   2   1

2 Circle the major 3rds.

3 Circle the minor 3rds.

4 Is the distance between a major 3rd larger or smaller than a minor 3rd?

28

The tonic triad in the key of A minor

You will remember from Grade 1 that a **tonic triad** is a chord made up of the 1st, 3rd and 5th degrees of a scale. A tonic triad in a minor key works like this too.

Here is the scale of A natural minor:

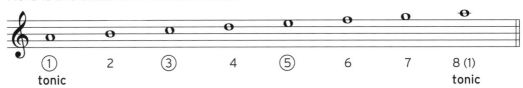

Here is the tonic triad in the key of A minor:

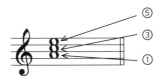

It is called a tonic triad in the key of A minor because it is built on the 1st degree (the tonic) of the A minor scale (natural or harmonic).

You will remember that major tonic triads are often labelled with a Roman numeral — I; minor tonic triads are labelled i. This shows that the chord is built on the 1st degree of the scale but that it contains a minor 3rd, not a major 3rd, at the bottom of the chord.

Composers sometimes label this chord as Am, especially if they are writing chord symbols for guitar.

In fact any chord that uses only the notes of this tonic triad (whatever the register) can have this label:

Chords and tunes that use only **A**, **C** and **E** fit together well – whether the chords or tunes are in the treble or the bass clef.

Handy tip!

Write Roman numerals below the stave(s).

i

Handy tip!

Write chord symbols above the stave(s).

Am

1 Add the missing notes to make tonic triads in the key of A minor.

2 The following music is all written using notes from the tonic triads that you know. In each case name the key. Then label the chord using a Roman numeral.

Key: _G major_   Chord: _I_

Key: _____   Chord: _____

Key: _____   Chord: _____

Key: _____   Chord: _____

Other minor keys – D and E minors

On page 23 you worked out that D minor is the relative minor of F major and that E minor is the relative minor of G major. These two keys are the other new keys you need to know for Grade 2. The tone-semitone pattern for their scales is the same as for A minor (natural or harmonic).

1 Write the key signature and tonic triad for each of the following keys.

Handy tip!
Look at page 42 to understand how these new keys fit into the circle of 5ths.

D minor   E minor   A minor

E minor   A minor   D minor

2 Write these one-octave minor scales in minims going up. The key signatures have been written in for you but you will sometimes need to add accidentals.

Remember
Relative minors share a key signature with their relative major.

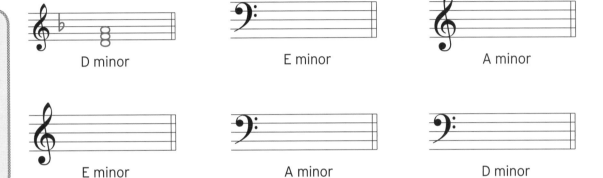

D natural minor scale

E natural minor scale

A harmonic minor scale

D harmonic minor scale

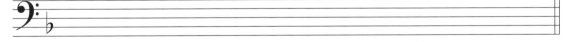

E harmonic minor scale

3 Write these one-octave minor scales in semibreves going down. Use key signatures.

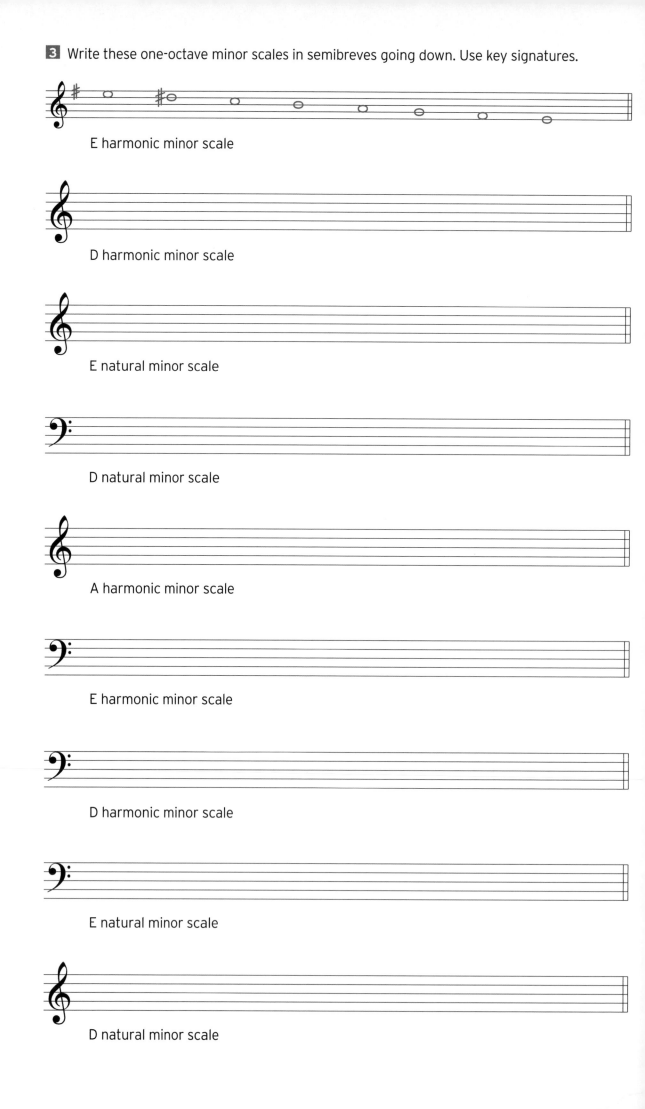

E harmonic minor scale

D harmonic minor scale

E natural minor scale

D natural minor scale

A harmonic minor scale

E harmonic minor scale

D harmonic minor scale

E natural minor scale

D natural minor scale

Labelling scales

1 Label these scales. Then write triads on the tonic and label them with Roman numerals.

A natural minor scale going down

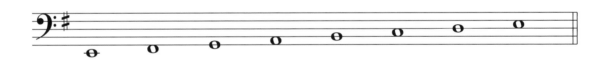

2 Label these scales. Here there are no key signatures so check the accidentals instead. Then write triads on the tonic and label them with chord symbols.

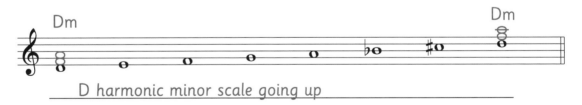

D harmonic minor scale going up

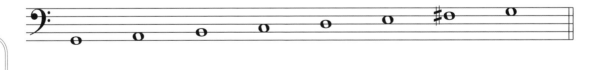

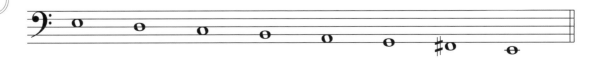

First inversions of tonic triads

Until now you have written tonic triads in **root position** (with the tonic (or root) at the bottom of the triad).

For Grade 2 you also need to be able to write tonic triads in **first inversion**.

Here is a tonic triad in C major in root position:

If the triad is 'inverted' so that the third of the chord is at the bottom (e.g. the root is put up an octave), the triad is in **first inversion**.

Here is a tonic triad in C major in first inversion:

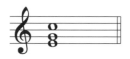

1 Write the key signature and tonic triad in root position for each key shown.
Then write its first inversion.

D minor

Tonic triad   Tonic triad
in root position   in first inversion

C major

Tonic triad   Tonic triad
in root position   in first inversion

E minor

Tonic triad   Tonic triad
in root position   in first inversion

A minor

Tonic triad   Tonic triad
in root position   in first inversion

G major

Tonic triad   Tonic triad
in root position   in first inversion

F major

Tonic triad   Tonic triad
in root position   in first inversion

Minor arpeggios

Here is the tonic triad in the key of D minor:

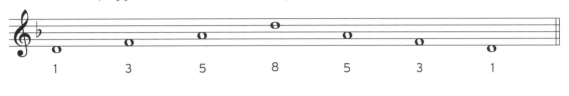

As with major keys, an arpeggio is made by 'breaking up' a chord like this and playing it as a tune. Here is the type of arpeggio that you need to know for Grade 2 – it is a one-octave arpeggio (shown here in the key of D minor).

1 Write the key signature and tonic triad for each key shown.
Then write its one-octave arpeggio in crotchets.

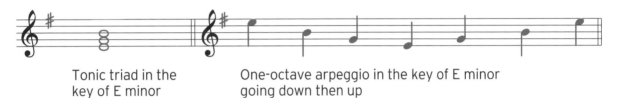

Tonic triad in the
key of E minor

One-octave arpeggio in the key of E minor
going down then up

Tonic triad in the
key of D minor

One-octave arpeggio in the key of D minor
going up then down

Tonic triad in the
key of A minor

One-octave arpeggio in the key of A minor
going down then up

Tonic triad in the
key of E minor

One-octave arpeggio in the key of E minor
going up then down

Labelling arpeggios

1 Label these one-octave arpeggios.

E minor arpeggio going up

_____

_____

_____

_____

_____

2 Put a bracket (⌐¬ or L_J) to show any complete one-octave arpeggios hidden in the music. Then name the arpeggio.

A minor arpeggio going up

_____

_____

_____

_____

Broken chords

Remember

An **accompaniment** is music that supports (or backs) a tune.

A broken chord, like an arpeggio, is made by 'breaking up' a chord.

There are lots of ways of making broken chords, depending on the rhythm you use and how many notes are used in each pattern. Here are some possibilities using the tonic triad in the key of G major:

Broken chords appear in all sorts of music. Composers use them to give music different textures and to make accompaniments sound more interesting. Sometimes you can find one-octave arpeggios within larger broken chord patterns.

Did you know?

Sometimes you can find one-octave arpeggios within larger broken chord patterns.

1 Using crotchets, write a broken chord using D minor tonic triad (going up). Use patterns of three notes each time. Finish on the first **A** above the stave.

2 Using quavers beamed in fours, write a broken chord using G major tonic triad (going up). Use patterns of four notes each time. Finish on the first **G** above the stave.

3 Using semiquavers beamed in fours, write a broken chord using E minor tonic triad (going down). Use patterns of four notes each time. Finish on the first **E** below the stave.

Working out the key of a piece

So far you have worked out the key of a piece of music by looking at its key signature (or its accidentals if there is no key signature).

For Grade 2 the music could be in a major key or its relative minor. As relative major and minor keys share a key signature you need to be careful.

Here are two examples showing how to work it out:

1

- Are there flats or sharps in the key signature? *Yes, one sharp, so the key could be G major or E minor*

- Are there any accidentals in the music that could be a raised 7th degree in the relative minor? *No*

- Are there any other reasons to think that the key is G major? *Yes, the first 2 bars are based around the tonic triad broken chord and the last note is G*

  Answer: *The key is G major*

2

- Are there flats or sharps in the key signature? *Yes, one flat, so the key could be F major or D minor*

- Are there any accidentals in the music that could be a raised 7th degree in the relative minor? *Yes (so the key is probably a minor)*

- Are there any other reasons to think that the key is D minor? *Yes, the penultimate bar centres around D and uses a raised 7th degree. The last note is D*

  Answer: *The key is D minor*

1 Use the questions above to work out the keys.

Beethoven

etc.

Key: _____

Haydn

Key: _____

Mozart

Key: _____

Purcell

Key: _____

Bononcini

Key: _____

Mozart

Key: _____

Haydn

Key: _____

Intervals – major and minor 2nds

Did you know?

Only the first of the following intervals is called a minor 2nd, even though the notes sound the same if you play them. This is because you must always count up from the bottom note using note names to get the interval number before you can say what interval it is.

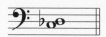

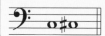

On page 27 you learned how to tell the difference between major and minor 3rds. For Grade 2 you also need to know the difference between **major** and **minor 2nds**.

Here is a major 2nd: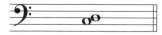

Interval: Major 2nd

(These notes can also be described as being a tone apart.)

Here is a minor 2nd: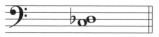

Interval: Minor 2nd

(These notes can also be described as being a semitone apart.)

In every major **and** minor key there is always an interval of a major 2nd between the 1st and 2nd degrees of the scale.

1 Circle the major 2nds.

2 Circle the minor 2nds.

3 Is the distance between a major 2nd larger or smaller than a minor 2nd?

Perfect intervals

For Grade 2 you need to know about **perfect 4ths, 5ths** and **8ths (octaves)**.

All major and minor scales have:

- a perfect 4th between the 1st and 4th degrees of the scale
- a perfect 5th between the 1st and 5th degrees of the scale
- a perfect 8th (an octave) between the 1st and 8th degrees of the scale

1 Name the following intervals.

Handy tip!

Ask your teacher to recommend some music to listen to with a lot of perfect intervals in it.

Interval: _Perfect 4th_

Interval: _____

Interval: _____

Interval: _____

Interval: _____

Interval: _____

Interval: _____

Did you know?

Violin, viola and cello players tune their strings so that there is an interval of a perfect 5th between each one; double bass players tune their strings so that there is an interval of a perfect 4th between each one. Most guitar strings are tuned in perfect 4ths too.

2 Name the following Grade 2 intervals.

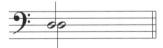

Interval: _Unison_

Interval: _____

Interval: _____

Interval: _____

Interval: _____

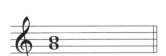

Interval: _____

Interval: _____

Interval: _____

Interval: _____

41

The circle of 5ths – major and minor keys

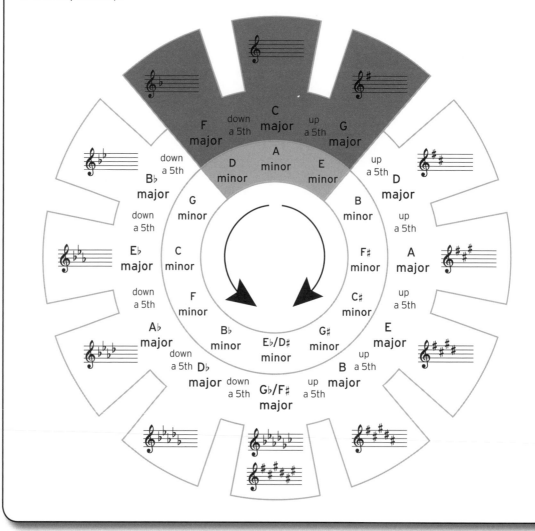

Here is the circle of 5ths including minor keys. The highlighted keys are the only ones that you will need for Grade 2.

Start at C major. To find the major or minor key with one sharp in its key signature just move round one notch to the right (or up a 5th from **C**) and the answer is there: G major (with its relative minor, E minor, below).

To find flat key signatures, move in the opposite direction. To find a major or minor key with one flat in its key signature just move round one notch to the left (or down a 5th from **C**). The answer is F major (with its relative minor, D minor, below).

Handy tip!

Now you will see that the 5ths in the circle of 5ths are perfect 5ths.

Using the circle of 5ths above, answer these questions:

1 Which minor key has one flat in its key signature?_____

2 Which major key has no flats or sharps in its key signature?_____

3 Which minor key has one sharp in its key signature?_____

4 Which major key has one flat in its key signature?_____

5 Which minor key has no flats or sharps in its key signature?_____

Sequences

A sequence is a tune pattern that is repeated starting on a different note. Here you can see that the second bar has the same tune pattern as the first bar but it is one note higher:

Some sequences are repeated at a higher pitch; some at a lower pitch.

1 Write a bracket (⌐‾‾⌐) above the sequences.

Did you know?

An ostinato repeats the rhythm to the same tune pattern. A sequence repeats the rhythm but also moves the pitch of the tune pattern.

2 Here is a section of a tune. Make a sequence by repeating it twice, one note higher each time.

3 Here is a section of a tune. Make a sequence by repeating it twice, one note lower each time.

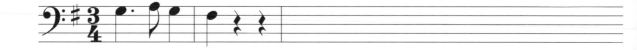

Transposing tunes up or down an octave

If a piece of music is written too high or low for an instrument to play – or for a voice to sing, it is sometimes necessary to move it to a more comfortable register. Look at this:

An alto (a low female voice) would find this easy to sing but it is too low for a soprano (a high female voice). **Transposing** it up an octave makes it comfortable for a soprano to sing:

You can also do the opposite to transpose a tune down an octave.

To transpose a tune up or down an octave:

- Look at the first note of the tune and find the next note with the same letter name (up or down depending which way you want to transpose the tune)
- Check this is correct
- Write out the tune with the same distances (intervals) between the notes
- Check that the last note you write has the same letter name as the last note of the original tune

1 Transpose these tunes up an octave to make them suitable for a soprano voice to sing.

2 Transpose these tunes down an octave to make them suitable for a bass voice to sing.

46

Musical words and symbols

A written piece of music can contain lots of information – not just the notes to be played and in what rhythm, but **how** to play it. For Grade 2 you need to know the following, in addition to the Grade 1 words and symbols:

Remember
Articulation marks are usually put close to the note-heads.

Articulation marks
(tell a player how to play the notes, e.g. smoothly or with an accent)

⌒ (phrase marks) – long curved lines written above the music that show its natural shape; they often relate to the number of notes that can be sung or played before taking a breath (even if the music is written for non-wind instruments). The signs · and // are sometimes used to show the end of a phrase where there are no phrases marks above the music.

♩ _ (_tenuto (ten.)_) – slightly lengthen and sustain the note

Handy tip!
Expression marks are usually put below the music.

Expression marks
(tell a player what kind of feeling/mood to give the music)

cantabile – with a singing tone

espressivo – expressively

grazioso – gracefully

molto – very (_molto espressivo_ means 'very expressively')

Register
(tells a player at which octave to play)

_8_ or _8ᵛᵃ_ (ottava above the notes) – play the music an octave higher, usually in keyboard music

_8_ or _8ᵛᵇ_ (ottava below the notes) – play the music an octave lower, usually in keyboard music

Remember
Tempo marks are usually put above the music at the beginning of a piece.

Tempo marks and other signs
(tell a player what speed to play the music and other details)

Adagio – slow

Allegretto – quite fast but slower than **Allegro**

M.M. ♩ = 92 – metronome markings

⌢ (pause mark) – hold the note or rest a little longer than usual

Vivace – fast and lively

| 1. | – first time bar |
| 2. | – second time bar |

1 Show that this music should be played gracefully. Add dynamics to show that it should be played softly. Add *tenuto* signs to the minims and add a phrase mark to show that this music is to be played as one phrase.

2 Show that this music should be played fast and in a lively way. It should be played an octave higher than written. It should be played loudly and the quavers should be slurred in fours.

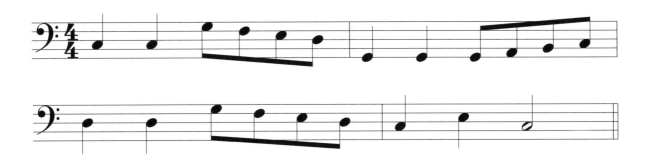

3 Show that this music should be played slowly and with a singing tone. Add *tenuto* marks to the dotted crotchet and to the minim.

4 Show that this music should be played at a moderate pace. Add dynamics to show that it should be played loudly. Accent the minims and add a phrase mark to show that this music is to be played as one phrase.

5 Show that this music should be played very expressively. It should be played at a walking pace and an octave lower than written. It should be played medium loudly and there should be a pause on the last note.

1 Write a tune using notes of the tonic triad in any register to the given rhythm. Use a key signature and finish on the tonic.

E minor

C major

D minor

F major

A minor

2 Write a tune using the first five degrees of the scale in any register to the given rhythm. Use a key signature and finish on the tonic.

E minor

F major

A minor

G major

D minor

3 Look at the tunes you have written and add some musical words and symbols that you know. Also see page 48 for those for Grade 2.

Analysis

1 Look at the following piece and answer the questions below.

> ### Remember
>
> Analysis is about noticing how music is composed. This helps you to play your instrument (or sing) more fluently because you understand how the music is put together.

> ### Remember
>
> Bar 1 is not usually numbered; the number is included here to make it easy to find the bar you need.

1. Name the note with an accidental in bar 3. _____C sharp_____

2. What note is the tonic in this piece?_____D_____

3. In which key is this piece?_____D minor_____

4. Circle this rhythm each time it comes: ♪ ♩ ♪

5. What is the musical word that describes the rhythm pattern that you have circled in question 4?_____Syncopation_____

6. Look at the first three notes in bar 1 and the first three notes in bar 5. What is different about the pitch?___The pitch in bar 1 is an octave higher than in bar 5____

7. Why are the semiquavers in this music beamed together in groups of four?
   ___The beat is a crotchet so they are beamed to match the beat_____

8. Look at the semiquavers in bar 6. What is the musical word that describes the use of the notes of the tonic triad in this bar?_____Broken chord_____

9. Put a bracket (⌐‾‾⌐) above each of the three sequences in bar 3.

10. How many notes higher or lower are the sequences in bar 3 repeated?
    ___Two notes higher each time_____

11. Name the interval between the two notes marked with asterisks (*) in bar 2. _Perfect 5th_

12. What does **Vivace** mean?_Fast and lively_____

13. The tonic is written in three registers in this piece. Circle an example in bar 6 of the lowest and the highest.

14. Write a chord symbol above the last note of this piece to show that the tonic triad should accompany it.

15. Describe the shape of this tune.

    ___Jumpy and wild, going up and down a lot_____

2 Look at the following piece and answer the questions below.

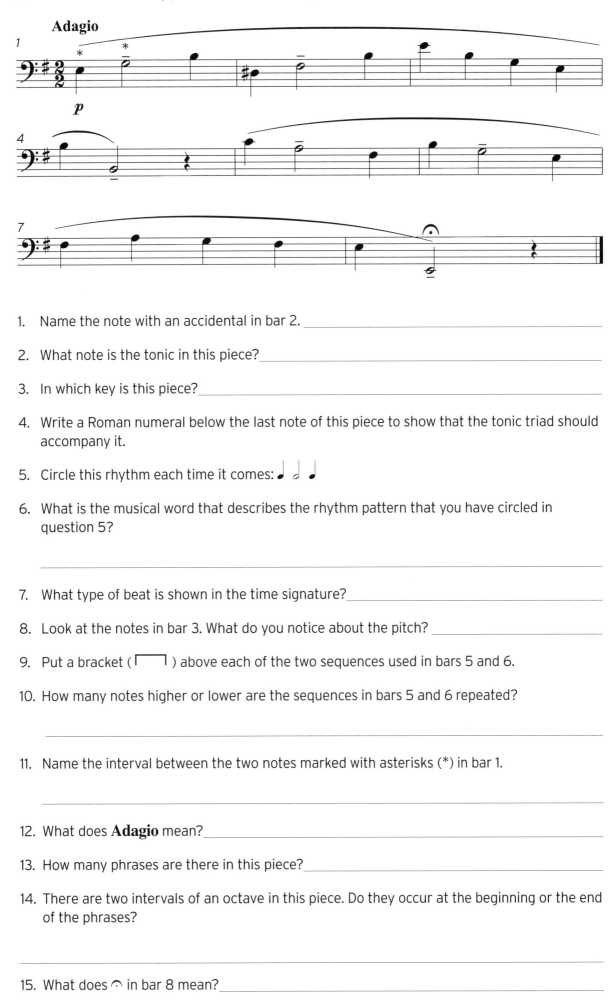

1. Name the note with an accidental in bar 2. _____

2. What note is the tonic in this piece? _____

3. In which key is this piece? _____

4. Write a Roman numeral below the last note of this piece to show that the tonic triad should accompany it.

5. Circle this rhythm each time it comes: ♩ 𝅗𝅥 ♩

6. What is the musical word that describes the rhythm pattern that you have circled in question 5?

   _____

7. What type of beat is shown in the time signature? _____

8. Look at the notes in bar 3. What do you notice about the pitch? _____

9. Put a bracket (⌐‾‾⌐) above each of the two sequences used in bars 5 and 6.

10. How many notes higher or lower are the sequences in bars 5 and 6 repeated?

    _____

11. Name the interval between the two notes marked with asterisks (*) in bar 1.

    _____

12. What does **Adagio** mean? _____

13. How many phrases are there in this piece? _____

14. There are two intervals of an octave in this piece. Do they occur at the beginning or the end of the phrases?

    _____

15. What does ⌢ in bar 8 mean? _____

3 Look at the following piece and answer the questions below.

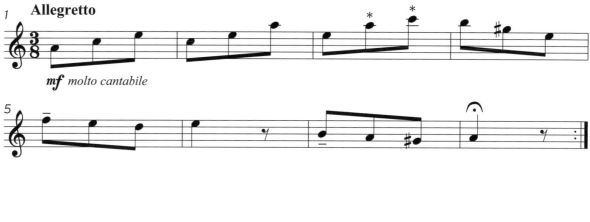

1. Name the note with an accidental in bar 7. _____

2. What note is the tonic in this piece? _____

3. In which key is this piece? _____

4. Write a chord symbol above the last note of this piece to show that the tonic triad should accompany it.

5. What type of beat is shown in the time signature? _____

6. What does **Allegretto** mean?

    _____

7. What does *molto cantabile* mean? _____

8. How should a musician play the first note in bar 7? _____

9. Look at bars 1-3. What is the musical word that describes the use of the notes of the tonic triad in these bars?

    _____

10. Put a bracket (⌐‾‾¬) above each of the two sequences in bars 5-8.

11. How many notes higher or lower are the sequences in bars 5-8 repeated?

    _____

12. Name the interval between the two notes marked with asterisks (*) in bar 3.

    _____

13. What does ⌑ mean? _____

14. Describe the shape of this tune. _____

    _____

15. What does ⅞ mean? _____

Section 1 (10 marks)

Put a tick (✓) in the box next to the correct answer.

Example

Name this note:

This shows that you think **C** is the correct answer.

A ☐ D ☐ C ☑

1.1 Name this note:

C natural ☐   C sharp ☐   A natural ☐

☐

1.2 Which is the correct time signature?

$\frac{2}{2}$ ☐ $\frac{3}{2}$ ☐   ₵ ☐

☐

1.3 For how many crotchet beats does this note last?

1½ ☐   3 ☐   2½ ☐

☐

1.4 Add the total number of crotchet beats of silence in these rests.

=

9½ ☐   6½ ☐   7½ ☐

☐

1.5 The relative major of A minor is: C major ☐   G major ☐   F major ☐

☐

1.6 Which sentence is correct?   D minor is the relative minor of C major ☐

The most closely related minor key to each major key is its relative minor ☐

F major has one sharp in its key signature ☐

☐

Trinity Guildhall reserves the right to alter the format and content of examination papers at any time. Please ensure that you consult the latest syllabus and our website – www.trinityguildhall.co.uk – before entering for an examination.

Put a tick (✓) in the box next to the correct answer.

1.7   The correct label for the following scale is:

D natural minor scale going down ☐

D natural minor scale going up ☐

A natural minor scale going up ☐

1.8   Which chord symbol fits above this tonic triad?

Em ☐   G ☐   Am ☐

1.9   Name this interval:

Major 2nd ☐   Perfect 4th ☐   Minor 3rd ☐

1.10   The following is:

A minor tonic triad in root position ☐

A minor tonic triad in first inversion ☐

C major tonic triad in root position ☐

Section 2 (20 marks)

2.1   Write a one-octave G major scale in semibreves, going down. Use a key signature.

2.2   Using quavers beamed in fours, write a broken chord using D minor tonic triad (going up). Use patterns of four notes each time. Finish on the first **A** above the stave.

Section 3 (10 marks)

3.1   Circle five different mistakes in the following music, then write it out correctly.

Section 4 (10 marks)

4.1   Here is a section of a tune. Make a sequence by repeating it twice, beginning one note lower each time.

Section 5 (15 marks)

5.1   Transpose this tune up an octave to make it suitable for a soprano voice to sing.

Section 6 (15 marks)

6.1   Write a tune using the first five degrees of the scale of E minor in any register to the given rhythm. Use a key signature and finish on the tonic.

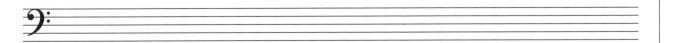

Please turn over for Section 7

Section 7 (20 marks)

Look at the following piece and answer the questions below.

7.1   In which key is this piece? _____

_____

7.2   Write a Roman numeral below the last note of this piece to show that the tonic triad should
        accompany it.

7.3   What does *molto cantabile* mean? _____

_____

7.4   At what speed should a musician play this piece?_____

_____

7.5   Comment on the phrase lengths in this piece. _____

_____

7.6   Put a bracket (⌐¬) above each of the two sequences used in bars 5 and 6.

7.7   How many notes higher or lower are the sequences in bars 5 and 6 repeated?

_____

7.8   Describe the shape of this tune. _____

_____

7.9   What does :‖ mean? _____

_____

7.10   Put a box (☐) around an example of an interval of a perfect 5th in the piece.